JavaScript

JavaScript Coding For Complete Novices

SCOTT BERNARD

Table of Contents

Table of Contents

INTRODUCTION

Congratulations on purchasing *JavaScript: JavaScript Coding For Complete Novices,* and thank you for doing so.

The following chapters will discuss some of the basics that you should know in order to get started with the JavaScript programming language. This is such a great language to learn how to use, especially if you are working on web pages and want to make sure that the add-ons are going to work in the proper way. It has a simple syntax and design that makes it easy for you to use, even as a beginner. This guidebook is going to help the beginner get started, so that they are able to write some code all on their own.

We are going to start this guidebook with some of the basics of JavaScript, such as how you will be able to use it and what it does. Then we will move on to writing commands inside of JavaScript, before talking about the JavaScript variables, how to teach the computer to make decisions without you being there, working with objects, and even how some of the operators work inside this coding language. When you are all done, you will have plenty of examples of how to write out your own code, and you will be able to use these as examples to work by yourself as well!

While working with coding language can be a challenge, and most of those who are not experienced with coding may find that it is scary to get started, there are so many things that you are going to love about this code. You will be able to read through it as a beginner, and as you will learn from this guidebook, most of the more complicated tasks are easy enough for a beginner to work with. Take some time to look through this guidebook and learn how to make some of your own codes, even some that are pretty complicated, whether you have experience with coding or not!

There are plenty of books on this subject on the market, thanks again for choosing this one! Every effort was made to ensure it is full of as much useful information as possible. Please enjoy!

CHAPTER 1

What Is The JavaScript Programming Language

There are many great programming languages that you are able to work with when you first want to learn how to do coding. And while learning how to do coding can seem like a lot of work, and troublesome for those who aren't used to it, it really doesn't have to be that difficult in the first place. You simply need to pick the coding language that you want to work with, learn a few of their basic commands, and you are ready to go. Coding can be exciting, and it isn't too hard to learn how to do, even if you are brand new to the experience and have no idea where you should start.

In this guidebook, we are going to talk about how to use the JavaScript programming language. This is a programming language that works well on various websites, and it is usually done in a manner as an add-on to the website. Many times you will use it alongside the Java programming language, and they both share much of the same library, commands, and more. If you already know how to use Java, you are probably going to be fine with JavaScript.

There are many reasons why you would consider working with JavaScript language when you are learning how to code. There are a wide variety of languages that you could learn and making the decision for your needs is never easy. With that being said, JavaScript is easy to learn how to use and it has a lot of the power that you want to make your websites easy to use. Some of the benefits of using the JavaScript programming language compared to some of the others includes:

- The execution happens on the client side: this makes it easier to have a faster speed compared to some of the other coding languages. Your work is not going to be limited based on the bandwidth of your own system. The client can do the execution on their own system and your information through the code will show up quickly for them.

- Easy to learn: there are many coding languages that are hard to learn because there are so many complex rules to learn or they are hard to read.

JavaScript is really easy to work with, especially if you have worked with Java in the past.

- Fast: when you are using JavaScript, you will notice that it is speedy and the information can get sent through fast. The user will have your code show up on their system within seconds, rather than having to wait around for the system to load things up.

- Simple: while there is a lot that you are able to do with the JavaScript program, it is still really simple, which can be nice for those who are just beginning to learn how to use it. You can learn the commands quickly, you will be able to read through the information, and you can pick what you want to add into the system in a short amount of time, even if you aren't used to coding.

- Works online: JavaScript is a coding language designed to work with the web pages that you are creating. This can be helpful if you would like to add in some videos or other similar options onto the webpage that you are working with. It will also work well with the web pages that are designed with Java so you can get even more functionality out of that.

- Versatility: there are many projects that you are able to work with on JavaScript. But if there happens to be a project that you can't get to work with JavaScript that you would still like to see happen, this coding language has the power to combine with another coding language. When the two power up, you will have the benefit of really seeing how strong the JavaScript programming is.

Now, while you are going to get a lot of benefits with JavaScript, there are a few negatives that you should watch out for. First, the security of JavaScript is not as strong as you will find with a few of the other options. This is because the execution is going to happen on the client side and many times this can result in someone sending over data that shouldn't be there. The developers of JavaScript are working on enhancing security, so this shouldn't be as big of an issue as before.

You will also find that this is a coding language that is going to be limited to working with things online. If you are creating a web page and need to put a little add-on into the system, this is the method that you will use to get that done. But for creating your own web pages, you will need to combine the Java program and another coding language to get the work done. JavaScript also doesn't work that well for writing your own programs outside of the web pages to ensure that you will get the stuff done that you want.

In addition, when it comes to working with JavaScript, the code is mostly going to be placed into the header of your web page. You can do a few different things with JavaScript to place it into the body of the page, or the header and the body of the page, but for the most part you will be limited to putting the code that you write into JavaScript right in the header.

Overall, the JavaScript program is going to be a great one to work with and can help you to get your own web pages set up in no time. Let's take another look at JavaScript and learn more about how this one is going to work for all your web page add-on needs.

Downloading JavaScript

Before we go more into some of the things that you are able to do with the JavaScript language, let's take a few minutes to take a look at how you can set up this language and get it to work on your own personal computer. During this process, make sure that you download an environment for JavaScript to work inside so that it is able to do its job. Eclipse is a good environment to work with, and it is easy to install and work on your computer. The steps that you must work on to get the Eclipse system to work include:

- Get on the internet and look for the eclipse download link on their website. It is often best to work with the newest version, so that you are able to get all the best features. Also, check to see which version is going to work the best on your computer.

- Once you find the link that you are going to use, it is time to open up the link to get it downloaded to the computer. You can also choose which directory inside the computer will be used for your workspace.

- The command prompt should then ask you about creating a new directory. Name it something that you will remember and then click OK to continue.

- When you reach this point, it is time to navigate to File, New, Static, Web Project. There should be a link that shows up that will open your dialogue box. Put in the name of the project, and then click on the button that says finish.

- Take a look on the left side of your environment and see that you will be able to click on a tab called WebContent. This is going to allow you to open up an HTML inside the current project. Just go to New and then to HTML and this will open the dialogue box that you need to get started with all of this.

At this point, the Eclipse system should be on your computer, so you can now spend your time taking a look through the JavaScript library. As a beginner, this library is going to really help you. A lot of the codes that you use in the beginning will be present inside of this library for you to have fun with. This will include the syntaxes, the terms, and so much more that you can look up and use whenever you need. It becomes much easier to write the codes that you want, to get the beginning syntaxes that you want to use, and to do so many other things when you are first getting started with this coding language.

When looking through this library, you should notice that the library for JavaScript is similar to what you will find with Java. If you already know how to work inside of Java, or you are learning JavaScript and Java at the same time, you will see that having these coding languages be similar can really make things easier to handle.

Remember that while we are going to use the Eclipse environment in this guidebook, because it is simple to download, has a lot of the features that you want, and it works pretty well with JavaScript, there are many other choices that you can make when it comes to environments. You can look around and see if there are others that you would like to use. You will find that many of them are going to work similar to the Eclipse system, and you should be able to use them the same as this one when writing down some of the codes inside this guidebook.

Once you have the JavaScript environment all set up and ready to use, and you have had some time to mess around and learn how it is going to work, you will be able to get started with your first project. Here you will be able to go into the Eclipse environment, or any of the other environments that you choose to use with JavaScript, open up your text box, and then get the document of HTML prepared. Once these are open, it is time to write out any of the codes that you would like to use and see how the programming works for you.

CHAPTER 2

Learning How To Make Some Code With JavaScript

The first chapter spent some time talking about why you should choose to go with JavaScript and how you will be able to get the environment primed to write codes inside. Now that all of this is set up, it is time to start learning how to make some codes inside of the environment, so you can really see how this program is going to work.

As a beginner, you may be worried about how you will start writing the codes. You may have seen some codes before, and you may feel like they are too impossible to start working on. You might think that since you are not able to read code right now, how are you going to be able to get out there and write some of your own. Luckily, the JavaScript language, as well as many of the other languages for coding out there have made some changes to ensure that writing and reading codes can be easier than before. By the time you are done, you will find that writing your own codes in JavaScript is much better.

When it comes to JavaScript, it is important to remember that you are working in a slightly different form of coding, the HTML form, rather than for making games or the other versions offered with options like Python or C++. Because you are working with an HTML language, you will need to make sure that you are using tags and that they are located in the right place inside the language. These tags are going to vary based on what you are trying to get the code to accomplish, but they are all going to work in similar ways to help you to get things done.

The basic syntax of using these codes is <script> and then at the end it would be </script> Keep in mind that the word script can be replaced with other things based on the different commands that you are trying to give to the coding language. Just remember that the slash mark is important if you would like to end the code that you are writing, and that the portion that doesn't have the slash is going to be how you begin the whole thing. Let's take a look at how this works for writing code and how you will be able to make it work for your needs.

There are a lot of different commands that you will be able to write out inside of JavaScript, but you need to make sure that they fit into the syntax that you have above, regardless of the commands that you are working with inside of this language. This chapter is going to take some time to look at how you would write out a code inside the JavaScript language as well as some of the things that you are able to do to make a difference with your coding, such as writing out comments, starting the code, and more.

Writing my code

Understanding what is going on above may seem a bit confusing when you first start, so this section is going to take some time to look at how it should all work together. We will show an example of a code inside of the JavaScript language, so take a bit of time to look at how it is outlined, what parts are present so you can start to see how some of your coding will look when it is your turn to start writing.

```
<!DOCTYPE html>

<html>

<head>

<meta charset- "ISO-8859-1">

<title> My First JavaScript Program </title>
```

```
</head>

<body>

        <script language = "javascript"
type = "text/javascript">

        document.write("Welcome to JavaScript First
        Program");

        </script>

</body>

</html>
```

There is a lot of information that is going on inside of this code and as a beginner, you may find that it doesn't make that much sense to you. Now it is time to start going through and breaking up this code so that you can have a better idea of what is going on in between each of the parts.

What does this code mean?

With the code that we are using above, the portion that states you are using JavaScript is going to be right in the body of the code. You should place this in the body many times so that the compiler knows what you are working with. For this particular code, the attributes are going to be declared as soon as the code comes up on the client's side when the web page loads.

So when the client uploads the web page where this code is located, they are going to get the message, "Welcome to JavaScript First Program." This is the output of the code, and it is what the computer is going to show the user. You are able to change or modify this saying in any way that you want to have it work on the web page, but for now we will keep it simple.

White space

When it comes to working on a coding language, you always need to be careful about the white spaces that are present. This can include the white spaces that are in between the words that you write or it can be the line spaces to separate things. Each coding language is going to read these white spaces in a different manner. Some will see them and assume that they mean something important, so you need to be really careful about what you are writing and how much space you leave between them. Others won't see this difference, and this allows you some freedom with the spacing because it makes the code much easier to read through.

When you are working on JavaScript, the spaces and the line breaks are not as critical as you will find with some of the other coding languages. They are there to help make the code easy to read and work with, but you could go without them and just write out your whole code on one line. Most programmers like to add in more white space for the reasons listed above.

It is a good idea to always leave in more white space than you think you need. Over time you will find a balance of what looks the best on your screen, but if you type in the codes too close together, you are running the risk of others not being able to read what is there. Adding in too much white space is going to be easier to read than too little, and as a beginner it is always better to place in more than you need until you get used to the system.

Using the semicolon

Another thing that you may have noticed in the code above is that there are some semicolons. Within the JavaScript program, the semicolon is not as important. You will often find that it is located after the statement has been written out, but it is more an idea of good practice between programmers rather than something that will determine whether the program is going to work in the compiler or not. You should add it in after the statements are done, but if you happen to forget, the compiler is still going to give you all the execution that you are looking for.

Case sensitivity

There are two patterns that can come up when you are working on your programming language. Some of the languages will notice that there are differences with the upper case and your lower case letters. These languages will read the words Book and book as two separate things. Other languages will be able to see Book and book and think they are the same. When it comes to the JavaScript language, you are going to have to be careful about the case sensitivity that you are working with. Make sure that you pay attention, because if you type in the wrong one with your functions, you will find that it is almost impossible to find that one later on. Always double check which case you are planning on using and then stick with that.

Comments

Comments are another important thing that you can work on when you are using the JavaScript language. These are going to help you to explain what is going on inside of your program without having the compiler make a mess within your system. If you would like to explain what you want the parts to work on, you need to add in certain symbols to make it happen. The programmers who look at your code will be able to look through the comments and see your notes, but the compiler will see the symbols and will just skip right over them to another part.

The nice part is that you are allowed to have as many of these comments inside of your code as you would like. For the most part, you should be careful about how many of these you are adding in, because if you have too many throughout the code, things can start to get a bit confusing. You may soon find that your code is much harder to read.

There are a few different things that you are able to do in order to write the codes that you want to use. These are going to vary based on the type of comment that you would like to use, as well as if the comment is going to take up one line or two lines. Some of the symbols that you are able to use when it comes to leaving comments in JavaScript include:

- Single line: if you are going to write a comment that is a few words long and won't take up all that much space. All you would need to do is put in the (//) symbols in order to write out these single line comments.

- Multiple lines: there are times when the comments that you would like to write are going to take up more than one line. If you use the symbols that were above, the compiler is going to try and read the part of the comment that goes to the second line. This doesn't mean that you aren't able to use a comment that goes over the one line, you just need to use the right one. Place the symbols </*>...<*/> to have your comment take up as much room as you want.

- HTML comments: it is also possible to write out HTML comments. This one is not going to take up as much space and will work for either the single line or the multiple line comments. You would just need to use the symbol <! To make one of these comments.

Writing out the comments inside of your code does not have to be difficult. As long as you place your symbols in the right place, the comments can be a lot of help without making it impossible to get the code to work. The following code is going to show you a few of the ways that you are able to use comments properly:

```
<!DOCTYPE html>

<html>

<head>

<meta charset = "ISO-8859-1">

<title>JavaScript Comments</title>

</head>

<body>

        <script type = "text/javascript">

        <!—The opening sequence single line comment.
```

> *The closing sequence HTML comment//--*
> *>*

> *// This is a single line comment.*

> */**

*This is a multiple line comment in JavaScript

*/

> *</script>*

</body>

</html>

Take some time to place this code into your program. Because it is going to be full of comments, there wasn't anything for the compiler to take a look at and nothing should appear on the screen. If something does show up on your screen, there must be a mistake in what you have written in the code. You may want to try adding in a few statements to see what the difference can be like, but this one is showing all the different ways that you will be able to input comments and how they are going to work inside of your code.

CHAPTER 3

What Are Some Of The JavaScript Variables?

There are a lot of different parts that you are able to work on when you are creating your JavaScript code. You will need to have all of these in place if you would like to make a great code, but learning each of the parts on their own, before combining them together, will make a big difference in how well you understand them. In this chapter, we are going to look at how you can write out variables inside of JavaScript.

The variables are basically the parts in JavaScript that will have a value, and they are only going to have this value once you assign it. They are going to be the different kinds of characters that you use inside of the code. The nice thing about this is you will be able to make the variable equal to any value that you would like, as long as you set it inside of the compiler. There are a few types of data that are available for you to use when you are working on the variables inside of your code. Some of these data types include:

- Text: this is the type of data that will be a sequence of words that then make up a statement. If you would like the program to say something on your screen when the user enters information, it would be done with the text variable. You could keep it something simple like, "Hello!" or you can make it something longer like, "Thank you for visiting my page. Come back soon!"

- Numbers: you can turn your variables into a number. You would be able to make a choice between using whole numbers or decimal numbers inside of the code to make it work the way that you would like.

- Boolean: the third data type that you are able to use in your JavaScript variables are the Boolean variables. These are going to work on a true and false basis and will be based on the information that you place into your code. For example, these are helpful if you would like something to come up on the screen only if the input is considered true.

One thing that you should keep in mind when using the JavaScript language is that there is going to be hardly any difference in the floating point or integer values that you are using. You will find that JavaScript doesn't see a difference between these, and you will be able to use them the same inside of your code. You won't have to spend much of your time worrying about how they work inside of the code.

Working with your variables

For the most part, you will see that the variables inside of JavaScript are going to be pretty easy to work with. When working with these variables, you should remember that they are the containers that you are using to hold all the data inside the code. You will be able to choose how you are using these containers and what information is going to go inside each of them. The thing that you need to remember here is to use the perfect keyword, which is going to be the "var" keyword in this language, so that you can tell the compiler that you are working with variables at this time. It also helps the compiler to know the container that it should bring out for you to use.

It is fine if this seems a little bit difficult to understand right from the beginning. Here is a good example of a code that uses the variable keyword so that you can see how things are going to work for your needs:

```
<!DOCTYPE html>

<html>

<head>

<meta charset = "ISO-8859-1">

<title>JavaScript Variables</title>

<script type = "text/javascript">

var name = "Appy";

var age = 21

var salary = 10000, expenses = 12000;

alert("Name:" +name + "Age:" + age + "/nSalary:" +
salary

                    +"Expenses:" + expenses)

    </script>

    </head>

    <body>

    </body>

    </html>
```

Despite this code not being all that long or big, there is actually quite a bit of information that you can find inside of it. When you look at the variable, you will need to start out with the variable initialization. This is going to help you to create a new variable that has a value attached to it. You can also do this when you choose to use the variable, rather than at the beginning of your code. The syntax that we listed above is the one that will make it easier to bring up some of the variables that you want to use, such as age, name, and salary. Keep in mind that you are able to use as many of these variables as you would like based on how you are setting up the code.

When you are working with the code above, there are several variables that you will notice and the user will be able to place the input that they want inside of there. For example, the user could choose to put in any answer that they want when the system asks what their age is. When this particular code is executed onto the screen, using the inputs that are placed in the code above, the following information is going to be the output:

Name: Appy

Age: 21

Salary: 10000

Expenses: 12000

Learning the scope of your variable

The next thing that we will discuss about your variables is their scopes. This is going to make a difference as it determines where the variable is going to be located and where you are able to see that variable within the code. It is going to help you to find where the variable is located and can give you a bit of control over who has permission to see these variables as well. There are two types of scopes that can be placed on the variable and these include global variables and local variables:

- Local variables: the first type of variable that you will work with are the local variables. These are the ones that you will only be able to see when you look at their exact location inside of the code. You will not be able to see them anywhere else, which can help to give you a bit of security with the code and makes it easier to set up the parameters for that particular variable.

- Global variable: the other variable that you are able to use. With this option, you will be able to see the variable at any point, rather than just in its regular location. This kind of code is viable for anyone to change it, which could cause issues if you would like to make sure that everything stays the same. They will be present in many locations inside of the HTML document.

When you are choosing which of these two variable types that you would like to use, you should make sure that they are given names that not only help you to determine what is in them, but also that the names are not similar. For example, if you have a variable that is local as well as global, you should name them separate things, otherwise the program is always going to choose the local variable over the global variable.

Naming the variable

While we have spent some time learning about the variables and how they work within your system, it is also important to learn how you should name them. Naming the variables may seem simple, but it is important that you do it the proper way to help the program work the way that you want. You don't want to end up naming the variable the wrong thing and creating an error down the road. Some of the things that you will need to keep in mind when naming your variables include:

- Pick a name that makes sense: there are a lot of names that would be cool for a variable, but if you look at the name later on and have no idea what it holds inside, it is probably not the best name to choose. Go with a variable name that tells you what is inside and makes it easier to find and use the variable later on.

- Keep away from the keywords: in every programming language that you can use, there are some keywords that are reserved for giving commands. If you use these as the names of your variables, you are going to have some trouble because the compiler will get confused at what you are using. Make sure to stay away from the reserved keywords in JavaScript when you are naming your variables.

- Keep away from numbers: while you are allowed to use numbers within the name of your variable, you are not allowed to use them to start out the name. You can write out the name of the number so that it is all letters, but no numbers are allowed at the beginning. Start out the variable name with a letter or an underscore, and then the rest can be any combination of numbers, letters, and underscores that you wish.

- Remember that when you are writing out the name of the variable that they are going to be case sensitive. There are differences between the upper case and lower case in this language so make sure to use them properly or you may confuse the compiler or not get the results that you want.

If you are able to remember some of these simple rules inside of your variables when you are naming them, you will find that it is easier than you can imagine to name some of the variables. These rules help you to get the results that you want, help you to remember what the variable is holding, and even ensures that the other programmers who are working in your program have an idea of what the variable is doing.

During this time, you may want to go through and assign the value that you would like to go with the variable you are working on. The variable is empty if you don't add in a value that is going with it. The nice thing here is that you get some freedom in terms of the value that you would like to assign. You can keep it simple and give the variable a number as a value or you can give it a word, such as a color, a name, or something else that will be assigned to the variable. The value that you will assign to your variable is going to be different based on what you would like to get done within the code that you are writing.

Working with variables is important when you are inside of the JavaScript programming language. They are going to help you to do some classification within your programming and can help you to store different categories together all in one place. As long as you learn how to use the variables in the correct way, using some of the codes that are available inside this chapter, and you name the variables the right way, you will find that the variables are going to work out perfectly for your needs.

CHAPTER 4

Teaching Your Computer How To Make Decisions Without You

One of the neat things that you are able to do with the JavaScript coding language is to teach your program to make decisions, even if you are not there. You will not be present when the user is putting in their inputs, especially if a lot of people use the program. How can you make sure that the right answers are going to show up on the computer once the user places their input? For example, what if you put in a program that asks the user what their age is and you just want to allow people who are 18 or older onto the site? You could set it up so that the computer will allow someone in if they pick that their age is 18 or over, and you can even take it further and have the program list out another response if they put in an age that is less than 18.

There are so many things that you are going to be able to do with your system and it will all depend on the results that you are looking to get. Your job will be to list the criteria that you want the computer to follow, and then the system will wait to get the input from the user before deciding if that input meets your criteria. It sounds complicated and like it is going to be something tough to learn, but while it does add in a lot of power and more possibilities for what you can do on the system, it is easier to use than you would imagine.

When you are working with these kinds of statements, you are working with what is known as conditional statements. There are a few types that you are able to use depending on what you would like the system to do for you. For example, you could just have the system show up a result if the user puts in the particular input that you want, you could set it up so that it will have an answer regardless of what the user inputs into the system, and so much more. There are a lot of possibilities that you are able to play with when it comes to making decisions. It is just up to you how you work with them.

There are four types of conditional statements that we are going to learn about in this chapter, and each one of them will work to tell the computer how to behave based on the set of conditions that you put in place. The four that we will talk about in this guidebook include:

Switch case statements

If statements

If...else statements

If...else if statements

As mentioned, all of these are going to work in different ways to help you get the computer system to work how you want. There are a lot of options that come with using these, and we will take some time to talk about a few of these conditional statements in the following passages.

Switch Statements

The switch statement is the option that you choose to help the compiler to select from a list of block codes that it needs to execute. The switch expression is going to be evaluated just once, and then the value of this expression will be compared with the values that you can find in each of the cases. If it finds that there is a match between the expression and the values in the cases, the block of code associated with the case will execute. You can also set it up so there is a default. This basically means that if none of the cases match the switch expression, the default will be the part that runs.

Let's take a look at how the switch statement can look. We will use cases in order to run through the days of the week and each one will be given a number. We will have 0 for Sunday, 1 for Monday and so on. Here is how the code would look:

```
switch (new Date(). getDay()) {

        case 0:

                day = "Sunday";

                break;

        case 1:

                day = "Monday";

                break

        case 2:

                day = "Tuesday";

                break

        case 3:

                day = "Wednesday";
```

```
        break;

case 4:

        day = "Thursday";

        break

case 5:

        day = "Friday";

        break;

case 6:

        day = "Saturday";

}
```

So if your switch statement ends up being 2, the result or the output will be Tuesday in this case. The break keyword is an important one to have in the code. It is going to break out of the switch block which means that it will stop the execution of more code and case testing. If you didn't have the break in there, the code would still take some time to figure out if the rest of them will work or not. You most likely don't want the case testing to keep on going if the input is 0 because this can take some time to go through it. You can go without this, but it is best to have this in there because it can save you a ton of time in executing the code because it will find the answer and move on.

Another thing that you can add into your code is the default keyword. This one is going to specify what you would like to have run if there isn't a case match based on what is in your code. If you just had two or three days of the week on the previous code, you would use the default to take care of what happens on the other days of the week if they are chosen. Let's take a look at how this works in the following code:

```
switch (new Date() .getDay()) {

        case 6:

                text = "Today is Saturday";

                break;
        case 0:

                text = "Today is Sunday";

                break

        default:
```

```
        text = "Looking forward to the weekend";

}
```

In this example, if the person puts in a number that is not 6 or 0, they are going to get the result "Looking forward to the weekend" to come up on the screen. But if they choose 0 or 6 as their answer, they will get that as the output.

Using your if statements

The next conditional statement that we will take a look at is the *if statements*. These are some of the most basic of conditional statements, so of course they are some of the best to work with when you are getting ideas down on JavaScript. These are going to take a look at the specific conditions that you set up ahead of time on the system, and then look to see if the input of the user is going to match up to these conditions.

In this case, if the user puts in information that is considered true based on your conditions, the program is going to execute in the manner that you want. This could be in the form of a statement or message that goes out to the user. But, if your user puts in an input that proves false based on the conditions that you set in the code, nothing is going to happen on the screen. At this time, there will not be any messages or other things that come up on the screen because the input does not meet your condition. Later we will talk about how to change things so that you are able to make statements and messages come up whether the input is considered true or false.

Let's take a look at how this is going to work by using the age of the user. You may set up a program that is for voting. You will need to separate people out between whether they are under the age of 18 or 18 and older. You can use your "if" statement in order to set up your conditions so that the statements will come up when the user states that they are at least 18 years old. For example, if the user states that they are 41 years old, the statement would be considered true in this situation and your message, such as, "You are allowed to vote! Here is information on your nearest polling station!" would come up on the screen.

But, if your user puts in an age that is under 18, such as listing that they are 17, the system is going to find that input is false based on your conditions. With the if statement, the screen would just stay blank, and they wouldn't get any information or any statements from this answer.

Now that you understand how the basic if statement is going to work inside of your system, let's take a look at a good code that will show how this works and explain a bit more why the if statement can be so useful.

```
<!DOCTYPE html>

<html>

<head>

<meta charset = "ISO-8859-1">

<title>Basic IF Statement</title>

</head>

<body>

        <script type = "text/javascript">

        var salary = 10000;

        var expenses = 12000;

        if(expenses > salar){

        document.write("<b>Please either start
        earning more or spend less!</b>"):

        }

        </script>

        <p>We are inside the body
section...</p>

        </body>
```

</html>

Take the time to open up your compiler and type in the code to see what is going to happen. You can also type in a few of your own answers to try this out and see if your message will come up the right way or if you would like to make some changes to it. Make sure that you are trying out different options, such as some that would be considered true and some that would be false based on the conditions above, so that you are able to see how the system is going to react in both situations.

Using your if...else statement

As we mentioned a bit in the previous section, the if statement is pretty basic and you have probably already seen that there are some limitations to using it. There is only one right answer when it comes to the if statement, but if you look at the examples that we give above, no one wants to end up with a blank screen when they put in their age. They want to find out answers, and since they can't put in a number that isn't their age (or they shouldn't if they are being honest) this is not the most efficient method.

With the *if...else statement*, you get a bit more freedom with the answers that you are given. You can have an answer come up whether the input is considered true or false based on your conditions. If the answer is considered true, then you will have one statement or message come up on the screen, and if the answer is false, the second message or statement that you include in the code will come up for the system as well. There are many situations where the person may put in an answer that is true for them but not true for the conditions that you set out, and it is still good to have a response in place to tell the person why their answer may not be right or at least have something that shows up other than a blank screen.

There are a lot of ways that you are able to use this system. You are not stuck with just two options in here. Let's say that you want to make a program that will separate people into different ages. You could ask questions about your childcare center, and you want to separate out the ages of your children into different categories. For example, you could have categories for 0 to 3, 4 to 5, 6 to 8 and then 9 and higher. How are you going to handle this if you want to keep the information separated between these age groups, but you still want to have results come up on the screen?

The if...else statements will work on these. You are able to use the "else" to make this work as many times as you want. You are not limited to one time for this to work. Let's say that the person enters their age to be 10. The code is going to check and see if the age 10 works in the 0 to 3 group, and when that is false it will go over to the 4 to 5 age group and so on. It will finally see that the person fits into the last group, and then it will execute the message or the statement that you placed for that particular group of children. You can leave different messages inside each of the age groups and when the if...else statement determines that the age that is entered fits into one of these groups, that is the statement that will show up on the screen.

You can technically do this for as many of the age groups as you would like, but as a beginner you will probably want to keep this down to a bit simpler process. Here is a good example of how the if...else statement is going to work inside of JavaScript, so you can get a bit of experience with seeing this and writing it all out:

<!DOCTYPE html>

<html>

<head>

<meta charset = "ISO-8859-1">

<title>If Else Statement</title>

</head>

<body>

>*<script type = "text/javascript">*

>*var salary = 12000;*

```
var expenses = 10000;

if(expenses > salar){

document.write("<b>Please        either        start
earning more or spend less!</b>"):

}

else {

        document.write("<b>You   have   enough
        money to spend!</b>");

</script>

        <p>We     are     inside     the     body
section...</p>

</body>

</html>
```

With the example above, we are keeping it easy to work with, just including in one of the else parts to make it easier to learn how to do. Remember that you will be able to add in more statements and make it longer if it works for what you would like to do inside your code. This is going to add in more of the freedom that you want with your code and can make it pretty powerful to use. However, you should start out slowly and build up.

If...else if Statements

The last statement that we will cover here is the if...else if statement. This one is a bit more advanced than the if...else statement because it allows you to have several parts to the statement. It will allow JavaScript to make a decision based on more than one condition that the programmer sets. Basically, these are just a series of if statements where your if is going to be in the else clause from the previous statement. The statements will execute based on which one is true, but if none of the conditions end up being true, the else block will be the one that is executed.

Often this is a good one to choose if you would like to make a game that gives several options. The user would be able to pick from option 1, 2, 3, or more and whichever one they pick would give the proper statement. If they don't pick one of the options given, you could set that as the else part and get something like "That is not a valid answer" as the output to the user.

Let's take a look at how the if...else if statement will work inside of JavaScript with this example:

<html>

```
<body>

<script type="text/javascript">

 (!--)

        var book = "math";

        if(book == "history"){

        document.write("<b>History
Book</b>");

        }

        else if(book == "math"){

        document.write("<b>Math Book</b>");


        else if(book == "economics"){

        document.write("<b>Economics
Book</b>");

        }


        else{
```

```
            document.write("<b>Unknown      Book
</b>");

        }



        //→

    </script>
```

<p>Set the variable t different value and then try...</p>

</body>

<html>

In this example, we set the variable to be "math" so the output that we will get is Math Book. You will be able to set the variable to equal any type of book that you would like and one of the answers will come up for you. Try changing up the variable and see that it all comes out the way that it should for the output corresponding to the right book.

There are a lot of different ways that you are able to separate all this out to make it work inside the code.

You can work with ages, with numbers, with how much the user makes versus their spending, and so much more. As you get to writing more code, and get more experience with how the language operates, you will be able to find a lot of ways to use the if statements, if...else statements, and the if...else if statements in order to make your code look truly amazing.

The important step here is to take a bit of time to learn how to write out and create the conditional statements that we talked about inside of this chapter. This is going to help you to get the feel for how these conditional statements work, and you will be able to find new and creative ways to make them work inside the programs that you will want to write. You can have some fun with these codes, experiment with the answers that you want the users to give you, and learn exactly how to create your programs according to your needs. Have some fun, get a bit of practice, and don't be afraid to mess up – it's the best way to learn.

CHAPTER 5

Making Objects A Part Of Your JavaScript Tool Belt

Now it is time to move on to learning about the objects that are used inside of JavaScript. Most of the modern scripting languages that you will be using are known as object oriented programming languages. In the past, another form was used to help you learn how to code, but this could be complicated to understand and learn and many beginners found that it was easy for things to get messed up and moved around. To make things easier to work with, a lot of the newer coding languages worked out these bugs and went over to the object oriented type of programming.

While using this kind of programming language can make things a lot easier to handle, you still need to be careful about how you are using the objects in the system. The objects are going to be tied to real life things that are in your life, and you must check that you are using these objects the right way. If you don't use them properly, the compiler is going to have issues with executing the codes in the manner that you would like.

Inside the JavaScript language, the objects are going to be the parts of the program that you will use and each of your objects will have attributes that are there to define them properly. These may include things like the function of the object, and other times they would include the method. A good way to think about the attributes that go with the object is to think over how they act, look, and feel. Think of an object in your head, such as a ball. This is going to be the object inside of the JavaScript program. Now think of the features that you will associate with that ball. You could think that it is red, that it is big, and even some of the actions that it is going to take such as rolling or bouncing. These are going to be the attributes that are associated with your object.

You are able to put together as many of the attributes that you would want to go with the object, but you need to have them make sense. If someone looked inside the category of ball, they should not find something in there that wouldn't make sense for a ball. For example, it wouldn't make sense to give the feature of talking or hearing to a ball because most people would not give these attributes to the ball. All of the attributes that you add in need to make sense and fit with what you want to do.

You are able to do this with any object that you think of in this process. Whether you are thinking about a car, a dog, a person, a door, or something else, this is going to be the object that you are working with. Any of the features that would be used to describe this object would be the attributes that come with it. Inside of JavaScript, the object is going to work in a similar way, although it may not look like that right in the beginning. If you get confused with the way that the objects are working inside of this coding language, just make sure to think of it like we just did in this exercise, and it should all fit together again.

This chapter is going to take a bit closer look at how the objects work inside of your JavaScript programming so that you can understand how to use them and why they are so important inside of the code.

Understanding how the properties of the objects will work

So now we are going to take some time and learn a bit more about some of the properties that come with working with objects in JavaScript. There is a bit of diversity when you are working on the properties that go with your object. As the programmer, you are going to get some freedom when you are choosing the data types that go here, including getting to pick whether you would like to use Boolean values, strings, or numbers with your objects. You may find that sometimes the data type that you are using with the objects is going to be more abstract compared to other types.

Even though there is a lot of freedom with choosing the property that goes with the objects you are using, it is still important that no matter what property you choose, when it goes with an object, it is also going to be attached to the variable that is used whenever you create the object.

Another thing to keep in mind when you work with objects is that all objects will be considered global variables. This means that when a new object is created, you can see it throughout the code, rather than just in the one location where it was created by the programmer. This will happen each and every time that you place your object into the computer, as long as it is placed into the code in the correct way. This may seem like a hassle, but in reality having the object be a global variable will make it quite a bit easier for other programmers, including yourself, to find the information that they need when searching for the object.

Now that we have spent a bit of time talking about some of the properties that go with the objects in your code, let's take a look at a code that will use the object as well as some of their properties:

```
<!DOCTYPE html>

<html>

<head>

<meta charset = "ISO-8859-1">

<title>Objects Example </title>

        <script type = "text/javascript">

                objectName.objectProperty        =
                propertyValue;

                        var str = document.title;

        </script>

</head>

<body>

</body>

</html>
```

After you take time to place this code into the compiler of your system, you should see that it has already gone through and given the variable to the objects throughout the code. These are also going to be some of the locations where you will be able to place the objects when the code is being executed.

Is there a relationship between the methods and their objects?

When you are working in a coding language and the methods of the object is mentioned, it pretty much means that we are talking about the functions of the objects. The functions that you use to execute the objects need to be in place so that they can tell the object to behave in a certain way. The function does run slightly different compared to the method since the function is able to work as a statement and a standalone, while the method is always tied to a keyword within the code. It will always be tied to the action of that keyword, but there are times when they will be able to work in a similar manner.

For the case that was above, the method of the object is going to be used inside the syntax in order to display the contents of the object onto a HTML page. They will often use this to write out the various parameters that you want to have with the object method, but sometimes they will also include some of the operations that you want to use inside of your code. You can even use some of the methods, such as the write() method, to pass the text string on to the page, helping the user to see the string or the statement on the screen whenever that program is executed.

Showing the operator on the page

While we will spend some more time talking about operators and how they work within the next chapter, we are going to talk about them just a bit here. What is considered the new operator is going to be the one that you used in order to create a new instance inside of the object. If you are working to create this new object inside of the JavaScript language, you need to watch out to make sure that the new operator is going to be inside the code in the correct spot. If it ends up in the wrong spot, it is going to have some trouble executing properly and it won't work the way that you would like.

One of the tools that you should use to make these operators work properly in your code is the constructor method. You need to make sure that the function is being properly used within the code so that it works as well. For your new constructor method to work out the way that you would like, there are three main functions that will help. The three functions that help out with this issue include the object(), data(), and array() functions.

Now that we have talked about some of the parts of the object and even how to get the operators to show up on the screen, let's take a look at how you will be able to get these to work inside the code with the following syntax:

<!DOCTYPE.html>

```
<html>

<head>

<meta charset = "ISO-8859-1">

<title>The New Operator</title>

<script type = "text/javascript">

        var student = new object()

        var languages = new array

("JaveaScript", "Pascal", "Python");

        var day = new Date("August 24, 1989");

                alert (day);

</script>

</head>

<body>

</body>

</html>
```

At this point, you should take a moment to place this into the interpreter for JavaScript and see what will come up on the screen. If the code has been placed into the interpreter the proper way, when you go to execute this inside the HTML program, a little alert box should show up. This alert box is going to place the date that you listed inside (you are able to put in a different date than what is listed above if you would like to give this a try), along with the time and all the other information that we placed into the code. You can add in more information and make this as simple or complex as you would like depending on the information that should go into the alert box.

While you are working on the code above, why not take some time to make changes to the information that is inside? You can continue on with some of the parts that are already in the code or mess around a bit. See if you are able to add in some other parts based on what we have done in other chapters in this book. It can be a lot of fun to experiment and see what you are able to come up with, such as what is going to come up in the box, and you can have a lot of fun all at the same time.

As this chapter has pointed out, there are a lot of things that you are going to be able to do when you work with objects inside of JavaScript. While it does allow you to have some fun and allows for more to do inside the system, it is pretty easy to learn. The syntax that is in this chapter is a good one to use when you want to work with objects, but you are a bit confused on where to get started. Try it out a few times and see what you are able to do.

CHAPTER 6

What Are The Operators And Why Do I Need To Learn About Them?

In this guidebook, you will find that there are quite a few things that we have spent time learning about. We talked about the basics of writing down your commands to make them work, as well as about variables and how to assign values to them, how to use the if and the if...else statements, and even how to use objects properly inside of the system. All of these are important to ensuring that you are able to write out the codes that you want the most inside of your compiler.

But there is still a lot more that you are able to do with JavaScript, even when you are a beginner. In this chapter, we are going to spend a bit of time looking at things that are called "operators" in the JavaScript code. These are simple tools that you are able to use, but they are going to provide you with more power and freedom, as well as room to be more creative inside your own codes.

If you would like to add more power between your coding, it is time to learn how to use some of the operators. The operators are pretty easy to learn, but it is still something that you should spend some time on when you are first learning this kind of language. They are going to work to tell your code what you would like to do inside of the program, and there are even different types of operators that you are able to use based on how the code will react.

You are going to be surprised at how simple these operators are to learn when you find out what they are all capable of doing for you. They can help you to compare things, to assign values to some of your variables, and even to do some basic math inside of the program. Let's take some time to look over some of the operators that you are able to work with inside of JavaScript and see how they will be able to make a big difference in your coding results.

The arithmetic operators

As mentioned above, there are a few types of operators that you are able to use in your coding, and one of these is the arithmetic operators. This is the one that is going to help you to do math inside of the compiler. It can be as simple as adding two of your variables together or it can be a long string that will combine a few of the different symbols together to get the results that you would like. It is a good idea to learn how a few of these work to make sure that your variables will be treated in the right way. Some of the arithmetic operators that you may run across include:

- (+)—this is the addition operator and it is going to tell the code to add together two operands such as X + Y

- (-)—this is the subtraction operator and it is used in your code to subtract the second of your operands from the first one such as X − Y

- (*)—this one will be used as the multiplication operator and can be used in order to multiply two operands together such as X * Y.

- (/)—this is the division operator and it will be used in your code in order to divide the two operands such as X / Y

- (%)—this is the modulus which is the operator that will output the remainder of the integer division. You will show this by X % Y

- (++) this is the increment operator and it is going to increase the chosen integer by one. For example, you would use it like X++ and you would get X to be one higher than usual.

- (--)- this is the decrement operator and it is going to decrease the value of the integer by 1.

As you can see, these are pretty easy ones for you to use and they will make a big difference in some of the things that you are able to do with your code. In addition to using these just one at a time, remember that you can add in a few to each of your statements to make it more interesting. For example, you can choose to have a statement that uses addition as well as subtraction inside of it. You can use all of the operators in one or go with just a couple of the same one. There really aren't any limits when it comes to using these.

If you do happen to use more than one type of operator inside of your statement, you need to keep in mind that the order of operations is going to come into effect. This is basically that the system will look at the statement and take care of all the multiplication, and then the division, and then addition, and finally subtraction and it goes from left to right when it does this. It is a minor thing, but can make a difference when you are writing out how to use your arithmetic operators inside of the code.

The comparison operators

The second kind of operator that you are able to use inside of the JavaScript is the comparison operator. These are the ones that you will use when you would like to compare a value to your variable inside of the statement. There are a few signs that you are able to use to give this comparison over to the variable. Unless you have worked in coding in the past, you may not be familiar with what all of these mean. Some of the comparison operators that you are able to use and which are good to know about include:

- (==)—this is the equal operator and it is used to see whether the values your two operands end up being equal or unequal. If the values are equal, your condition is going to be true.

- (!=)—this is the not equal operator and it is going to be used to check out two operands and to see if they are equal or not. If the values are not equal, the condition is going to be true.

- (>)—this is the greater than symbol. This type of operator is going to be used to see whether the values of the left operand ends up being higher the one of the right operand. When the one on the left is greater, then the condition is true.

- (<)—this is the less than operator and it is going to be used to see if the operand on the left is less than the operand on the right side. If the left side is less than, the condition is true.

- (>=)—this is the equal to or greater than operator. It is used to see whether the values of the operand on the left side is equal to or greater than the value of the operand on the right side. If this is correct, the condition is going to be true.

- (<=)—this is the equal to or less than operator. This operator will be used to see if the operand on the left is equal to or less than the value of the operand on the right. If this is correct, the condition will be true

When you are working with the comparison operators, it is a good idea to remember that when one of the statements is false for the operators that are inside of that statement, the whole thing is going to be false. You could have twenty items inside of the statement and have 19 of those items be true, but if that last one ends up being false, then the whole statement is going to be considered false as well. This could help you out if you find that the system is not working the way that you would like.

The relational operator

The next type of operator that you may want to use inside of your coding is the relational operator. These are great for showing that there is a relationship that is going on between the values and the variables that are inside of the code. There aren't as many of these as some of the other operators that you would want to use, but they are still important to learn about for when you do need them. Some of the relational operators that you may want to learn about include:

- (!)—when used in JavaScript, this is the logical NOT. When you see this sign, it will mean that if your operands are non-zero, the condition is going to be false.

- (||)—when you use this operator, you are using the logical OR. This one means that if any two of the operands that you are using are non-zero, the operator is going to turn the condition into a true one.

- &&--when you see this operator, you will know that it is the AND operator. This one means that if both of the operands are non-zero, the operator is going to make this a true condition.

If there is a relationship that you need to have shown between your value and the variable in the code, you will need to make sure that you are using one of the three relational operators that are listed above.

The assignment operator

And finally, we are also going to take some time to talk about the assignment operators. These come into play if you are working inside a code and want to make sure that you are able to assign a value to the variable that you are working with. Keep in mind that the variable is all alone without any assignment until you pick a value that is supposed to go with it. There are a few different types of operators that are going to be used to do this, and some of these operators are going to be similar to what you find inside of the arithmetic operators, but you should be able to tell the difference between them based on the context that they are being used in. When working with assignment operators, here are a few of the most common symbols that you will utilize:

- (=)—this is the simple assignment and it is used to assign your right side value to the operand that is on the left side.

- (+=)—this is the add and assignment operator that will add together the right operand and the left operand, and then will assign this result to the operand on the left side.

- (-=)—this is the subtract and assignment. This works like the previous one. You will take the right operand and then subtract it from the left operand. The result is going to be assigned to the left operand.

- (*=)—this is the multiply and assignment where you will multiply the operand on the right with the one on the left and then assign the results to the left operand.

- (/=)—this operator will divide the operand on the left side with those on the right operand and then takes this result and assigns it to the left operand.

These are going to make it easier to take your variable and assign the right value so that it works each time that you would like to use it. This is a simple process and you should be able to get it to work so that all of the variables inside of your code will have the right value assigned to them. Without a value, the variables are just empty containers inside of your code.

As this chapter has shown, there are many different types of operators that are allowed inside the code. As long as you are using them in the proper way, you should be able to see some great things happen inside of your coding. They are there to show comparisons and to give assignments between the variable and its value. They are there to show relationships and to even make it easier to do some mathematical equations inside of your code. While they may be simple and are pretty easy to learn, you are sure to already see that there are quite a few uses that come with the operators in your JavaScript coding.

CONCLUSION

Thank you for making it through to the end of *JavaScript: JavaScript Coding For Complete Novices*. No matter your experience with coding in the past, you will find that JavaScript is easy to use and a lot of fun. You will be able to use it to make some cool things inside of your web pages. I hope it was informative and able to provide you with all of the tools you need to achieve your goals, whatever they may be.

The next step is to get started with writing some of your own code inside the JavaScript language. This is an easy language to learn, even for those who don't have any prior coding experience. It is easy to read, has a lot of power, and is going to allow you to do a lot of cool things inside of the websites that you are working on. When you add it together with the Java program, you will find that it is one of the best options that you are able to use for your programming needs.

Inside this guidebook, we learned a lot about the different things that you are able to do with JavaScript. After taking some time to look at the basics that are behind this coding language, we talked about some of the basic commands that are found inside of it, then moved on to the variables, how to teach the computer to make its own decisions, what the objects are inside of this language, and even what the operators are all about and why you need to learn about them. By the time you are done with this guidebook, you will have the knowledge that is needed to write some amazing code for your own needs.

Finally, if you found this book useful in anyway, a review on Amazon is always appreciated!